Book Description

Driving is not just a skill but a necessity for most people. When you drive you will not only be depending on your actions to drive safely, but also on other drivers who are making their decisions. It is for this reason that there are several regulations for driving a vehicle on roads. You need to have a certified driving license that people can verify easily. To get a legitimate driving license, you first need to write a knowledge test, and only when you pass the knowledge test will you be able to take the road test with an examiner. So, no matter how good you are behind the wheel, it is a must that you have a good knowledge of different road signs and rules.

Get It Done Right The First Time !

This book will help you achieve what you are hoping for. With more than 250 questions and with additional tips & skills from our experts you will be able to ace your test by practicing the questions and following the expert tips we have provided.

What will you learn from this book?

- Different road rules

- Road regulations

- Road signs

- Tips to remember the test content easily

- How to not be anxious during the exam date

And a lot more.

Practice Makes Perfect
USA DMV Written Exam & Skills Book

Yours Truly

Astrix Publishing House

Table of Contents

Introduction

In order to drive a vehicle in accordance with your state's rules and regulations, you must pass the Department Of Motor Vehicles (DMV) test. DMV tests consist of two parts: a knowledge test and a road test. Your knowledge of basic road rules, signs, and common sense will be tested in the knowledge test. A road test challenges your actual driving skills with the aid of an examiner. You must first pass your knowledge test according to your state's rules and regulations in order to take the road test. There are different question patterns used by different states, but all authorities use the test to measure how familiar you are with the basic rules that every driver should know.

How to Remember the Test Content Easily

Tests are tough but they help us to become better. The DMV test helps and prepares first-time drivers to drive with confidence on the road. While driving on the road, you are accountable for your actions. But also, you might be in danger because of others' actions or because of natural reasons such as weather conditions. To prepare for any situation along the way, the DMV helps you realize different hazardous situations that may affect your life or others.

By preparing for the DMV test, you are also preparing yourself to face these road situations without panic. To get the most out of the information provided in this book or official handbooks by the DMV authorities, you need to be sure to follow the memory techniques that can help you remember the scenarios, signs, and questions that are mentioned in this guidebook.

Memory Techniques to Ace Your DMV Test

1. Use Images

   Humans have the power to process visual information more easily than written text. When you practice a concept from the test material, try to create images for it or find some images that you can use to remember the concepts effectively. As road signs are easy to browse from the Internet, make it a habit to look at them at least for 30 minutes a day. To remember a topic vividly, we recommend creating images in your mind. When an image becomes ridiculous in your mind, it becomes easy to remember.

2. Use Acronyms and Mnemonics

   Acronyms are constructed from the initial components of a longer name or phrase. They can help you remember complex information easily. Mnemonics are the most popular memory techniques for students. Usually, a mnemonic is a tool that helps you remember large amounts of information with less effort. Group similar topics and questions to create mnemonics that make more sense.

3. Create a Story

   Use the content you have read to create a silly story in your mind. Storytelling is a popular cognitive technique to remember information vividly. Take some important concepts discussed in the material regarding road rules and use them to weave a story so you can remember them during the test.

4. Study in Different Locations

   To ensure that your brain is storing the information correctly, it is important to study in different locations. Visit a library or a coffee shop instead of learning all the time in your room.

5. Say the Information Out Loud

   You will be more likely to remember information if you try to remember the content as loudly as possible. Reading out loud increases the chances of encoding information into your brain.

6. Understand First Then Memorize

   Whenever you are trying to memorize a topic, you must understand it first. The simple rote learning method isn't efficient and will not help you remember for a long time.

7. Teach to Others

   Teaching the topics you have learned to someone who is unaware of the topic can help you improve your understanding of the subject. Teach them like they are five years old and you will grasp the concise depth that the subject provides.

8. Use Flashcards

   Flashcards are an easy way to remember information with the use of different colors and a few cards. You can also use mobile apps to create flashcards digitally. Flashcard creation is a memory management technique to not only remember content but also to connect all of the topics in an easier way. Flashcards can be used to memorize concepts and to learn deeper topics with more efficiency.

9. Use the Peg System and Memory Palace

Both peg and memory palace systems are often used by high-level memory contest competitors. Both of these techniques are used to remember the entire test content within a few weeks. A peg system often uses a few words to sum up all of the content. In contrast, a memory palace creates your own memory device inside your brain to easily encode and decode information.

10. Use Mind Maps

Mind maps are special diagrams that students and researchers use to map content to be revised instantly and easily. You can create mind maps using paper and pen or by using computer softwares such as MindNode and Xmind.

Apart from all the techniques mentioned above, it is also important for people trying to ace the DMV test to review and revise the questions they have practiced constantly.

Here We Go: USA DMV Questions

Question 1:

At a railroad crossing, you hear ringing bells or flashing red lights close to you. As a driver, what should you do?

A. It indicates that a train has just passed and hence, you are good to go

B. It means that a train is far away and you should proceed with caution

C. You need to take a U-turn and change lanes

D. It means that a train is approaching and hence, you need to stop at least 15 feet away from the tracks

Correct answer is **D**.

Explanation:

Whenever you see flashing red lights, crossing gates lowering, or ringing bells at a railroad crossing, it's a sign that a train is very close or passing. You should stop at least 15 feet before the tracks and proceed further only when the lights have stopped flashing and the crossing gates are fully raised.

Question 2:

A circular intersection where all the traffic moves in a counterclockwise direction is known as a:

    A. A divider

    B. A roundabout

    C. A merged lane

    D. A four-way intersection

Correct answer is **B**.

Explanation:

A roundabout helps drivers take the entrance at the intersection and exit at any street they want to. Roundabouts reduce traffic delays and help minimize accidents effectively.

Question 3:

You see a winding road ahead sign while you are driving. What should you do?

    A. Increase your speed

    B. Move at the same speed as you are currently driving

    C. Stop your vehicle for some time

    D. Slow down your speed and move with caution

Correct answer is **D**.

Explanation:

A winding road ahead sign is used when the road ahead has more than three curves. There are high chances of accidents in these curves and you need to take it as a warning sign and proceed with caution.

Question 4:

What should you do if an emergency vehicle such as an ambulance approaches you while sounding a siren?

    A. Continue with the same speed

    B. Slow down your speed and pull over to the left side of the road

    C. Make a sudden break and stop wherever you are

    D. Pull over to the right edge of the road

Correct answer is **D**.

Explanation:

When an emergency vehicle such as an ambulance or fire engine approaches with a siren, you should make sure that you stop your car at the right edge of the road. Only proceed further when you are sure that the emergency vehicle has passed.

Question 5:

What should you do when you see a downgrade board sign while you are driving?

    A. Take a U-turn

    B. Accelerate your speed and move with caution

    C. Slow down, shift to a lower gear, and use breaks

    D. Slow down, shift to a higher gear, and use breaks

Correct answer is **C**.

Explanation:

A downgrade board sign indicates that there is a steep descent ahead. Make sure that you are using brakes and shift to a lower gear. Look out for any vehicles such as trucks and proceed with caution.

Question 6:

To maintain a safe journey and avoid accidents, it is recommended to follow the:

  A. One-second rule

  B. Ten-second rule

  C. Three to four-second rule

  D. Two-second rule

Correct answer is **C**.

Explanation:

Rear-end collisions are one of the common ways for accidents to happen. To have a safe journey, leave at least three or four seconds of distance between you and the immediate vehicle. If the vehicle in front of you is a truck or any high-moving vehicle, then you need to increase the distance further for your safety.

Question 7:

You are on a steep mountain road, meet another vehicle going uphill, and you both can't pass. Which vehicle has the right-of-way?

  A. Vehicle traveling uphill needs to go first

  B. You should go first

  C. Neither vehicle is allowed to go

  D. The vehicle that arrived first should go

Correct answer is **A**.

Explanation:

On a steep mountain road, the vehicle going uphill always yields the right-of-way because the vehicle going downhill has more control while backing.

Question 8:

On a roadway with three or more lanes, which lane will provide smoother traffic for the driver? Which should you choose most of the time?

A. The left lane

B. The right lane

C. The middle lanes

D. The lane with less traffic

Correct answer is **C**.

Explanation:

When going on a roadway with more lanes, it is important to move in the middle lane if you want smooth traffic because the people in the right or left lanes sometimes wish to move into the streets of their respective sides, whereas vehicles in the middle lane go forward.

Question 10:

On interstate highways, which lane should the slower vehicles prefer to travel?

A. Left lane

B. Right lane

C. Middle lanes

D. Any lane with less traffic

Correct answer is **B**.

Explanation:

Except when passing, it is a rule that all slower vehicles on an interstate highway take the right lane.

Question 11:

How do you determine a slow-moving vehicle on the road?

    A. It will have a triangular orange sign on the rear of the vehicle

    B. It will have a red circle sign on the rear of the vehicle

    C. It will have a sign with "slow moving vehicle" on the rear of the vehicle

    D. It will have a sign with a triangular red sign on the rear of the vehicle

Correct answer is **A**.

Explanation:

All slow-moving vehicles like farm tractors and roadway maintenance vehicles have a triangular orange sign on the vehicle's rear. All slow-moving vehicles should not exceed 35 mph. If you are driving a slow-moving vehicle and there are at least five vehicles stuck behind you, then you need to pull over to let them pass.

Question 12:

Which of these should you not do when you are driving?

    A. Talking while using a handheld cell phone

    B. Texting while driving

    C. Use a wireless device even if it is not an emergency

    D. All the above

Correct answer is **D**.

Question 13:

What does a suspension of your driving license mean?

    A. It means you can drive only once a day

    B. It means your privilege to drive is temporarily revoked by the authorities

    C. It means your privilege to drive is terminated for an indefinite time

    D. It means you can drive only in the day

Correct answer is **B**.

Question 14:

What is the distance by which as a driver you are not legally allowed to park near crosswalks or crowded places?

A. 15 feet

B. 30 feet

C. 100 feet

D. 5 feet

Correct answer is **A**.

Question 15:

What should you do if someone waits to cross at a crosswalk?

A. Don't stop for the pedestrians

B. Stop and let them cross

C. Horn continuously

D. None of the above

Correct answer is **B**.

Question 16:

How often should you check your tire pressure?

A. At least once in three months

B. Once yearly

C. Whenever you are going on a long trip

D. At least once a month

Correct answer is **D**.

Question 17:

Suppose you have acute eye problems that force you to use contacts or glasses. What should you do when you are driving?

   A. Always wear them when you are driving

   B. Wear them only when there is high traffic

   C. Only wear them at an intersection

   D. Only wear them at night

Correct answer is **A**.

Question 18:

How do you protect yourself against carbon monoxide from the car's exhaust system?

   A. Make sure your car is ventilated

   B. Turn on the fan and check your exhaust system

   C. Open the window whenever it is necessary

   D. All the above

Correct answer is **D**.

Question 19:

When should you wear seatbelts while driving?

   A. Law requires you to wear seatbelts all the time when you are driving

   B. Only when you are traveling on an interstate highway

   C. When you are traveling at night

   D. Only if you are traveling above 60 mph

Correct answer is **A**.

Question 20:

How much distance must you be away from an airbag?

    A. 2 inches

    B. 5 inches

    C. 10 inches

    D. 4 inches

Correct answer is **C**.

Explanation:

You must stay at least 10 inches away from an airbag. If not, then there are chances of you getting seriously injured if there is a crash.

Question 21:

Suppose you have taken over-the-counter medication. What should you do before or while driving?

    A. Consult your doctor whether the new medication can affect your driving

    B. Be extra cautious and drive slow

    C. If you are having difficulty driving, stop your car to the right side of the road and wait for someone to pick you up

    D. All the above

Correct answer is **D**.

Question 22:

What is the speed limit in an active school zone?

    A. 50 mph

    B. 100 mph

    C. 25 mph

    D. 60 mph

Correct answer is **C**.

Question 23:

Which is a good driving skill among the below options?

    A. Managing space as a defensive skill while driving

    B. Driving fast when there is a lot of traffic

    C. Driving while listening to music with Bluetooth headphones

    D. All the above

Correct answer is **A**.

Explanation:

Managing space means leaving enough distance between you and the vehicles surrounding you. This skill can help you react quickly and escape safely whenever there is a crash or a nearby on-head collision.

Question 24:

To which emergency vehicles must you yield?

    A. Ambulances

    B. Fire engines

    C. Rescue vehicles

    D. All the above

Correct answer is **D**.

Explanation:

You must yield to all emergency vehicles if they are moving with a red siren. Not doing so is a legal offense.

Question 25:

What should you do if you start to cross an intersection on a freeway after making sure that there is no one around, but suddenly see someone entering the freeway?

A. Give room for the car entering the freeway

B. Block the car entering the freeway

C. Stop your car and wait for the car to enter the freeway

D. Move faster than you are driving

Correct answer is **A**.

Explanation:

Whenever you are on the road and you see a car traveling onto the freeway or an intersection, you should give room for it to enter. If *you* are entering onto a freeway, you should drive at the same speed you were traveling or according to the flow of the traffic after your observation.

Question 26:

Which is dangerous while driving?

A. Driving near parked cars

B. Driving fast near to a school zone

C. Driving while under alcohol influence

D. All the above

Correct answer is **D**.

Explanation:

It is important to stay cautious, especially when driving near parked cars, as there is a chance of the passengers opening the car door anytime.

Question 27:

Which rule should you follow when you are stopped at an intersection?

    A. Look left, right, then look left again before crossing

    B. Look left and cross

    C. Look right and cross

    D. Look right, left, then look right again before crossing

Correct answer is **A.**

Explanation:

You should first always look left, right, and left again because the traffic coming from the left will be closest to you and can be responsible for fatal accidents most of the time.

Question 28:

What of these should be followed before changing lanes?

    A. Check if there are any vehicles behind you

    B. Use your mirrors and turn your head to look to the sides

    C. Turn your signal on for at least 5 seconds before changing lanes

    D. All the above

Correct answer is **D.**

Question 29:

If you are traveling at 55 mph, how much space as a driver may you need for making a stop safely?

    A. 100 feet

    B. 50 feet

    C. 1,000 feet

    D. 400 feet

Correct answer is **D.**

Explanation:

It is best if you always make a close approximation of the space required for a stop according to your speed and other conditions such as poor weather, road condition, and traffic flow.

Question 30:

When should you use your horn?

    A. When your headlights are not working

    B. When you are bored

    C. When there is a potentially dangerous situation

    D. When you are changing lanes

Correct answer is **C**.

Question 31:

What should you do if you see a dangerous hazard such as debris on the road that may cause a fatal accident?

    A. Move as fast as you can

    B. Slow down and turn on your emergency flashers to alert the other drivers

    C. Take a U-turn and leave

    D. None of the above

Correct answer is **B**.

Question 32:

What should you do if a school bus stops ahead of you and the driver turns on its flashing red lights?

    A. You can move ahead

    B. You need to stop until the red lights stop

    C. You need to wait for other drivers to make your decision

    D. You need to horn continuously

Correct answer is **B**.

Question 33:

What should you do if a traffic ticket is issued to you without your mistake?

- A. Fight with the officer about the injustice
- B. Protest on the road and stop the incoming traffic
- C. Appear in a court and make a dispute if you are sure about your concerns
- D. Don't pay the fine

Correct answer is **C**.

Question 34:

Which of these are illegal according to the road rules?

- A. Blocking an intersection
- B. Parking your vehicle on a crosswalk
- C. Driving under the influence of alcohol or drugs
- D. All the above

Correct answer is **D**.

Question 35:

What happens if your license is revoked and you still drive a vehicle?

- A. Nothing will happen because driving is your right
- B. You will be making an illegal offense and can land in jail or may need to pay a hefty fine
- C. You will be given a warning
- D. You will need to pay a fine

Correct answer is **B**.

Question 36:

Which headlights do you need to turn on after sunset or before sunrise?

A. Low-beam headlights

B. High-beam headlights

C. You don't need to turn on headlights

D. Both low and high-beam headlights

Correct answer is **A**.

Question 37:

Which of the below is an offense?

A. Traveling in a vehicle not registered with any of the states

B. Changing lanes while signaling the other drivers

C. Traveling with an alcohol limit that is allowed

D. Traveling cautiously when there is a school zone

Correct answer is **A**.

Question 38:

If a police car approaches you with a siren behind you, what should you do?

A. Move forward, ignoring the signal

B. Stop suddenly wherever you are

C. Turn your right turn signal on and stop on the side of the road carefully

D. Take a U-turn and block the police car

Correct answer is **C**.

Explanation:

When a police siren approaches, don't panic, and use the turn signal to stop the car carefully on the right side of the road. Sometimes when the police stop you, it means that you may have a bad tire, or you may not be wearing your seatbelt. It is important to stop and hear out the issue. Don't argue with the officer if the problem was a mistake or wrong. Argue about it in court with a judge if the decision was unfair.

Question 39:

What should you do if you are involved in a minor collision with a driver?

   A. You shouldn't stop and should drive away from the place as soon as you can

   B. You should stop and check whether the driver is safe

   C. You should take a U-turn

   D. You should horn continuously

Correct answer is **B**.

Explanation:

While minor collisions are not fatal, you must check the condition of another driver. Most of the time, the driver will be in shock or anxiety will surround them. Make sure that they are fine and move ahead only after the confirmation.

Question 40:

What should you do if you enter a road construction zone?

   A. Drive fast

   B. Horn continuously to alert the workers

   C. Turn on your low-beam headlights

   D. Stop the vehicle

Correct answer is **C**.

Question 41:

What should you remember whenever you are in front of a large truck?

   A. They will take more time to stop

   B. They can increase their acceleration swiftly

   C. Large truck drivers don't need to follow traffic rules

   D. Trucks don't stop unless there is an emergency

Correct answer is **A**.

Explanation:

Due to their build features, it takes more time for large trucks to stop than smaller passenger vehicles such as cars and jeeps. So, you mustn't stop quickly if you are in front of them to avoid a collision.

Question 42:

Why is it recommended to adjust your driver's seat?

- A. For your comfort
- B. For helping passengers in the backseat to have more space
- C. To reach the pedals easily and to see the road more clearly
- D. All the above

Correct answer is **C**.

Question 43:

Which of these do you need to follow when driving?

- A. Have a complete focus on the vehicle in front of you
- B. Fix your attention only on the center of the road
- C. Both 1 & 2
- D. Neither 1 nor 2

Correct answer is **D**.

Question 44:

Which of these is a fatal legal offense according to traffic rules?

- A. Turning on low-beam headlights when you are entering a construction zone
- B. Turning on high-beam headlights when you are approaching another vehicle
- C. Turning on high-beam headlights on a rural road where there is less traffic
- D. Turning on low-beam headlights during the daytime

Correct answer is **B**.

Question 45:

What is the maximum speed allowed near a crossing railroad track?

  A. 15 mph

  B. 20 mph

  C. 50 mph

  D. 60 mph

Correct answer is **A**.

Question 46:

What should you do when driving in poor weather conditions?

  A. Drive as you do in normal weather conditions

  B. Drive recklessly

  C. Drive cautiously

  D. Don't drive at all

Correct answer is **C**.

Explanation:

Always be cautious because it takes more time to stop your vehicle during unfavorable weather conditions.

Question 47:

What should you do if you are in a safety zone and see people boarding a bus?

  A. Drive with caution

  B. Horn continuously

  C. Flash your headlights

  D. Wait until all of them safely board into the bus and the bus moves

Correct answer is **D**.

Question 48:

If you are traveling with a child under 12 years old, where should they usually be seated?

A. In the front seat

B. In the back seat

C. Either back or front seat

D. Child is not allowed to travel

Correct answer is **B**.

Explanation:

You must have airbags in your car and the child should be placed in the back seat for their extra safety.

Question 49:

Which one of these is correct if you are driving at excessive speeds?

A. High-speed driving provides you happiness

B. It increases the chance of crashes

C. It improves your driving skills

D. It doesn't cause any crashes

Correct answer is **B**.

Question 50:

What are blind spots?

A. Areas that you cannot see in your mirror

B. Areas that are exactly behind your vehicle

C. Areas that are opposite to you

D. None of the above

Correct answer is **A**.

Explanation:

Areas that you cannot see from your mirror are called blind spots. To see these spots, you need to turn your head and look over your shoulder, making it difficult, especially when there is a lot of traffic. These blind spots are usually called no-zones. Large vehicles have increased blind spots, making drivers be extra careful.

Question 51:

You are driving on the road at night when there is heavy rain. What should you do?

    A. Use your emergency red flashing lights

    B. Use your low-beam headlights

    C. Use your high-beam headlights

    D. Horn continuously to alert other drivers on the road

Correct answer is **B**.

Question 52:

When traveling on a slippery road, what should the drivers do?

    A. Move faster

    B. Stop the car and alert other drivers

    C. Take a U-turn

    D. Take turns more slowly than you usually do

Correct answer is **D**.

Explanation:

Slippery roads are common during winter seasons. Being extra cautious while taking turns is important.

Question 54:

What are the signs of a drunk driver?

    A. Driving cautiously

    B. Sudden stops

    C. Signaling before changing lanes

    D. Doesn't drive rashly

Correct answer is **B**.

Question 55:

As a driver, what should you do if you see fire under the hood of your vehicle?

A. Drive without worrying about the fire

B. Jump from your car because it is unsafe

C. Block the road for help

D. Pull the vehicle off the road safely and turn off the ignition before getting out of the car. Once you get out, call the fire department for help

Correct answer is **D**.

Question 57:

When you see a red traffic sign, what should you do?

A. Drive faster

B. It is a construction warning

C. It means that you should stop

D. It means that you need to warn other drivers

Correct answer is **C**.

Question 58:

Why are mirrors unreliable sometimes?

A. Because you will not be able to see blindspots in mirrors

B. Because they are not useful

C. Because they need to be adjusted while driving

D. Because they are broken easily

Correct answer is **A**.

Question 59:

Which of these options can an emergency vehicle do legally?

    A. Exceed the speed limit

    B. Hit the vehicles on their way

    C. Block the roads for a long time

    D. All the above

Correct answer is **A**.

Question 61:

If you see a "closed lane" board while traveling, what should you do?

    A. Ignore the sign

    B. Make a U-turn

    C. Look at the ongoing traffic and merge to the correct lane when it is safe

    D. None of the above

Correct answer is **C**.

Question 62:

The following distance of your vehicle can be increased in one of these conditions:

    A. Normal traffic

    B. Slippery roads

    C. Interstate highways

    D. Roundabouts

Correct answer is **B**.

Explanation:

As slippery roads can increase your chances of a crash, it is recommended to increase the following distance for your safety.

Question 63:

Which of the following is a better way to deal with tailgaters?

    A. Block their way

    B. Argue with them

    C. Let them pass if it's safe

    D. Honk your horn continuously until they stop tailgating

Correct answer is **C**.

Explanation:

Tailgaters are annoying. Even though it is not your mistake, sometimes they are the ones that are increasing your chances of a crash. It is better to let them pass.

Question 64:

Which of these can alcohol cause?

    A. Increased sight

    B. Improved mind awareness to make decisions

    C. Improved driving abilities

    D. None of the above

Correct answer is **D**.

Question 65:

You are driving on the road and you see a funeral procession approaching. What should you do?

    A. You should move without worrying about them

    B. You should yield the way to them as they have the right-of-way

    C. You need to yield the way only when there is a sign with them

    D. None of the above

Correct answer is **B**.

Explanation:

A funeral procession always gets the right-of-way. Should the leading vehicle enter an intersection, all the vehicles in the procession should follow it. Only when all the vehicles cross the intersection, other vehicles should move.

Question 66:

A sign that is colored orange signifies:

    A. A stop signal

    B. School zone signal

    C. Animals zone

    D. Work zone signal

Correct answer is **D**.

Question 67:

What should a driver do to prevent hydroplaning?

    A. Make sure that your tires are properly inflated

    B. Make sure to clean your car

    C. Make sure to horn continuously while driving

    D. Make sure to go at high speeds while it's raining

Correct answer is **A**.

Explanation:

Hydroplaning is a phenomenon that occurs when a layer of water acts as a barrier between wheels and the road surface, causing the vehicle to stop responding to control inputs. To ensure that your vehicle isn't affected by hydroplaning, make sure that tires are inflated and have good tread depth. It is also important to reduce the speed you drive when it is raining or when the road is filled with snow.

Question 68:

You are going at a high speed on a rural road and you see children playing on the road. Should you give space to the kids and pass slowly?

    A. Yes

    B. No

    C. Depends on the conditions

    D. Yes, but only when it is night

Correct answer is **A**.

Question 70:

Someone driving with a lack of sleep can cause fatal accidents as equal to a:

    A. Drunk driver

    B. Angry driver

    C. Teenage driver

    D. All the above

Correct answer is **A**.

Explanation:

Both fatigue and drinking have the same effect on the driver. So, it is advised not to drive under the influence of alcohol or without sleep.

Question 71:

A slow driver can never cause accidents.

    A. True

    B. False

Correct answer is **B**.

Explanation:

A slow driver will often have equal blame as a rash driver. Slow drivers can disrupt the flow of traffic and can cause hazardous accidents. You should never go below the speed limit unless permitted as a slow-moving vehicle. Even if your vehicle is slow-moving, you should yield to vehicles behind you if you are disrupting their way. Not doing so can be a legal offense in many states.

Question 73:

You are near an intersection and you see an officer directing traffic. What should you do?

    A. Follow the officer's instructions

    B. Follow the signals

    C. Honk at the officer for doing something illegal

    D. Look at your fellow drivers and do what they are doing

Correct answer is **A**.

Explanation:

Most of the time, you will be following signs or signals that exist on the road. But sometimes, such as if there is an accident or if the signal lights are not working, an officer will control the traffic and you should follow their instructions.

Question 74:

Which of these can cause fatal accidents?

    A. Alcohol influence

    B. Not following traffic signals

    C. Highway hypnosis

    D. All the above

Correct answer is **D**.

Question 75:

Highway hypnosis, a dangerous driving condition that can cause fatal accidents, usually results because of:

A. Having too much sleep the day before driving

B. Eating too much before driving

C. Staring for a long time, scanning the roads and other vehicles

D. Highway hypnosis doesn't exist. It's just a rumor

Correct answer is **C.**

Explanation:

Highway hypnosis is usually caused when you travel for a long time, scanning, stopping, and observing the vehicles behind and beside you. Continuous staring can make you zone out and lead to crashes. It is suggested to take rest breaks instead of driving continuously.

Question 77:

When you are driving long hours, which is a better idea among these to avoid drowsiness?

A. Listening to your favorite music

B. Drinking alcohol

C. Driving slowly

D. Taking stops for rest at regular intervals

Correct answer is **D.**

Explanation:

It is always recommended for drivers to take rest stops at regular intervals to avoid drowsiness. Not doing so can sometimes cause fatal accidents. Be safe now rather than being sorry later.

Question 78:

What happens if you drink coffee after drinking alcohol?

    A. Increases your blood alcohol concentration

    B. There will be no change in blood alcohol concentration

    C. This decreases blood alcohol concentration and hence, you can drive

    D. This will decrease blood alcohol concentration only if you have drunk less

Correct answer is **B**.

Explanation:

Remember that your blood alcohol concentration (BAC) will in no way become less if you drink coffee or any other beverages. It is advised not to drive if your BAC is more than the permitted limit for everyone's safety.

Question 79:

What should you do if you are unable to see through the windshield due to it being blocked for any reason?

    A. Turn on emergency lights

    B. Drive without stopping

    C. Take a U-turn

    D. Wait for someone to help you

Correct answer is **A**.

Explanation:

Driving without vision from the windshield is extremely dangerous. If you face this situation, turn on the emergency lights immediately to warn other drivers and park your vehicle safely on the side of the road.

Question 80:

Which of the below statements is true?

    A. Trucks are easier to drive

    B. Truck drivers don't need to follow traffic rules

    C. Trucks take more time to stop

    D. Trucks don't have breaks

Correct answer is **C**.

Question 81:

You can drive below the minimum posted speed limit during this condition:

    A. When there is no one around you

    B. When you are talking on a phone

    C. When it is raining and the roads are slippery

    D. All the above

Correct answer is **C**.

Question 82:

Which of the options should you do when you are merging onto the freeway?

    A. Drive slower than the flow of the traffic

    B. Drive faster than the flow of the traffic

    C. Drive near the speed of traffic

    D. Stop driving

Correct answer is **C**.

Question 83:

Which of these shapes is used for the speed limit sign?

    A. Round

    B. Square

    C. Pentagon

    D. None of the above

Correct answer is **D**.

Explanation:

The shape used for a speed limit sign is a vertical rectangle.

Question 84:

What does a steady red light mean on a traffic signal?

    A. Stop after the painted white line on the pavement

    B. Stop before the painted white line on the pavement

    C. Continue moving

    D. Stop only if there is more traffic

Correct answer is **B**.

Question 85:

What should you do when you see a flashing red light?

    A. Stop immediately

    B. Stop immediately only if there is an officer

    C. Stop immediately only if it is night

    D. Stop immediately only if it is raining and the roads are slippery

Correct answer is **A**.

Question 86:

What should you do if the traffic signals are not working?

    A. Treat it as a stop sign

    B. Continue moving

    C. Treat it as a stop sign only when there is no officer nearby

    D. None of the above

Correct answer is **A**.

Explanation:

It is safe to stop when the traffic signals are not working. Most of the time, an officer will reach the place immediately and control the traffic. Not doing so can cause traffic jams, especially when there is a lot of traffic.

Question 87:

Which of the following is true?

    A. When you see a flashing yellow arrow, don't enter into an intersection

    B. When you see a flashing red arrow, don't treat it as a stop sign

    C. When you see a flashing yellow arrow, enter into an intersection

    D. When you see a flashing yellow arrow, treat it as a stop sign

Correct answer is **A**.

Question 88:

What should the driver do if there is a steady green arrow?

    A. Yield to pedestrians and any vehicles still in the intersection

    B. Move without worrying about anyone

    C. Stop immediately

    D. None of the above

Correct answer is **A**.

Question 89:

What should pedestrians do if there is a "walk" sign?

    A. It means that they can walk safely at an intersection

    B. It means that they shouldn't walk

    C. It means they should walk only when there are no vehicles around

    D. It means they should walk only when there are other pedestrians

Correct answer is **A**.

Explanation:

A "walk" sign is the only way a pedestrian should cross at an intersection. Crossing the roads with no sign can be fatal and can cause accidents. However, remember that the drivers need to be extra aware during these situations and allow pedestrians to cross if they are stuck in the middle of the road.

Question 91:

What does a steady yellow X on a traffic signal mean when you are in a lane?

    A. It means that you can use the lane

    B. It means that the driver cannot use the lane

    C. It means that the lane is about to be closed to traffic and the drivers need to vacate the lane

    D. None of the above

Correct answer is **C**.

Question 92:

What does a steady red X on a traffic signal mean when you are in a lane?

    A. It means that you are not allowed to use the lane

    B. It means that you are allowed to use the lane

    C. It means that you need to vacate it as soon as possible

    D. It means that you need to make a U-turn

Correct answer is **A**.

Question 93:

What does a steady green arrow over a traffic lane mean?

    A. It means that you can use the lane

    B. It means that you shouldn't use the lane

    C. It means that the lane is only available for experienced drivers

    D. It means that the lane can be used only when there is sunlight

Correct answer is **A**.

Question 94:

Which signal will appear if the lane is only available for left turns?

    A. Steady white one-way left-turn arrow

    B. Steady white one-way right-turn arrow

    C. Steady green arrow

    D. Steady red X

Correct answer is **A**.

Question 95:

What should you do if a STOP sign appears?

    A. Move immediately

    B. Make a complete stop and wait for the officer for instructions

    C. Make a complete stop and wait for other drivers to make their decision

    D. Make a complete stop and move only after making sure that the intersection is clear without any vehicles and pedestrians crossing

Correct answer is **D**.

Question 96:

STOP signs are usually of which shape and color?

    A. Green pentagon

    B. Red octagon

    C. Red pentagon

    D. Red square

Correct answer is **B**.

Explanation:

In all the states, the STOP sign is an octagon shape and red color. Different countries may have different regulations. So, if you are traveling on special borders, you need to be aware of their signs for the STOP signal.

Question 97:

It is okay to lose your right-of-way privilege during which situation?

    A. When it can prevent accidents

    B. When it can help you reach your destination faster

    C. When it helps you to get a good name in society

    D. None of the above

Correct answer is **A**.

Question 98:

What is the speed limit at a blind intersection?

    A. 2 mph

    B. 20 mph

    C. 15 mph

    D. 100 mph

Correct answer is **C**.

Question 100:

Suppose you are involved in an accident that involves a death. What should you do?

    A.   Escape as far as you can

    B.   Make a written report to the concerned authorities or DMV

    C.   Talk with your family and decide whether or not to report to DMV

    D.   Talk with your lawyer and decide whether or not to report to DMV

Correct answer is **B**.

Question 101:

Seat belts are not effective.

    A.   True

    B.   False

    C.   Partially true

    D.   It isn't easy to decide whether it is true or false

Correct answer is **B**.

Question 102:

What should you do if a traffic officer orders you to drive even when a red light is on the signal?

    A.   You should not do it

    B.   You must look at what other drivers are doing then make a decision

    C.   You must do it

    D.   You must call traffic authorities

Correct answer is **C**.

Explanation:

You should always follow the traffic officer's instructions, irrespective of what signal or situation you might be in. Officers provide instructions to ensure safety on the road for drivers.

Question 103:

What does an arrow mark usually represent as a road signal?

    A. To stop immediately

    B. To call someone related to traffic authorities

    C. To slow down your vehicle

    D. To help you decide which lane you must turn

Correct answer is **D**.

Question 104:

You are near a railroad track and you see a line of traffic crossing these tracks. There are no signals or officers or gates nearby. What should you do?

    A. Pass the vehicles while they are trying to cross

    B. Stop your car and block other cars from going

    C. When your turn comes and even if you see a train coming, cross the tracks

    D. Before trying to cross look at the surroundings, make sure that no vehicle is nearby

Correct answer is **D**.

Explanation:

Usually, there will be gates or signals for most railroad tracks. However, sometimes when you observe no signs or gates, it is important that you be alert and cross the traffic when no nearby trains are passing by.

Question 105:

Which is true when you try to make a left turn from a one-way road into another one-way road?

    A. Move into the right lane and make a turn

    B. Move into the right lane, stop your vehicle immediately, and move only when there is no traffic

    C. Move into the left lane or to the left side of the single lane while trying to make a left turn

    D. None of the above

Correct answer is **C**.

Question 106:

If you see a signal board that is a vertical rectangle, what should you expect from it?

    A.   School zone ahead

    B.   A speed limit board

    C.   You need to stop your vehicle immediately

    D.   It is a board that describes in detail about the driving laws

Correct answer is **D**.

Question 107:

Which of the following statements is correct?

    A.   Airbags are meant to replace seat belts

    B.   Airbags are meant to fix seat belts

    C.   Airbags are meant to work with seat belts

    D.   Airbags are meant to protect seat belts

Correct answer is **C**.

Question 108:

One of the below statements is wrong.

    A.   Wearing seat belts is better for the driver

    B.   When driving in tough situations that are caused by bad weather, you should try to decrease the following distance with other vehicles

    C.   Always follow traffic signals and signs

    D.   Always give way to emergency vehicles that are driving with a red light

Correct answer is **B**.

Explanation:

During conditions with bad weather, you must maintain a certain distance to ensure no accidents occur.

Question 109:

One of the following signals represents driving with caution. What signal is it?

- A. Red signal
- B. Flashing yellow light
- C. Green signal
- D. Flashing red signal

Correct answer is **B**.

Explanation:

Whenever you see a flashing yellow signal, it is important to observe your surroundings and drive cautiously. This signal is often used to alert the driver that there will be a change in the traffic signal or a lane being closed.

Question 112:

Which of the signals direct drivers to services such as rest stops?

- A. Yellow and green
- B. Green and red
- C. Blue and white
- D. Brown and white

Correct answer is **C**.

Question 113:

On a yield sign, the letters are of which color?

- A. Green
- B. Brown
- C. Yellow
- D. Red

Correct answer is **D**.

Question 114:

You are on the road and you see a bus on the same side trying to make a left turn when you are trying to make a left turn. What should you do?

A. Make the turn first because you have the right-of-way

B. Call the traffic inspector

C. Ask the bus driver to know what should you do

D. Slow down and wait until the bus takes the left turn

Correct answer is **D**.

Explanation:

You must understand that large vehicles take more space and time to turn when on the road. Let them cross first during turns instead of going along with vehicles such as buses and trucks for everyone's safety.

Question 115:

Which of the following statements is wrong?

A. Drink alcohol when you feel sleepy while driving

B. Don't take rests while driving long hours

C. Take marijuana while driving at night as it increases concentration

D. None of the above

Correct answer is **D**.

Question 116:

You are traveling on an interstate highway and you see a sign that mentions a speed limit of 60 mph. What should you do?

A. Drive at 70 mph

B. Drive at 40 mph

C. Drive at 100 mph

D. Drive within the speed range of 60 mph always

Correct answer is **D**.

Explanation:

Speed limits help all vehicles have a smooth flow while traveling. In some states, you will be charged if you are either above or below the speed limit. So, it is important to be in the speed range while traveling.

Question 117:

Which one of the below options should you do before you start a vehicle?

A. Always make sure that the parking brake is set

B. Check whether the brake pedal is fine

C. Check whether the accelerator is fine

D. All the above

Correct answer is **D**.

Question 118:

All the regulatory signs are of which shape?

A. Diamond

B. Hexagon

C. Vertical rectangle

D. Horizontal rectangle

Correct answer is **C**.

Question 119:

When you see a sign with a deer on it, what should you do?

    A. Call the traffic authorities

    B. Drive faster because the deers may attack you otherwise

    C. Watch carefully and drive because sometimes the deer may cross the road

    D. Wait for the deer to cross the road. Until then, don't drive

Correct answer is **C**.

Explanation:

It is quite common to see signs with deer on it, especially if you are driving in hilly regions. Moving slowly when you see these signs is important because deer may suddenly cross the road. To avoid accidents or to not hurt the animal because of a collision, it is important to be aware of the surroundings by constantly scanning.

Question 121:

What should you do if you encounter a rash driver?

    A. Compete with them by racing

    B. Block their way using your driving skills

    C. Get out of their way

    D. None of the above

Correct answer is **C**.

Explanation:

Rash drivers are common, especially on rural roads. To not get hurt because of them, it is important to get out of their way and inform any traffic officer nearby about their rash driving.

Question 122:

Which of the following statements is true?

    A. You can park on a sidewalk

    B. You can park within an intersection

    C. You can park on a crosswalk

    D. None of the above

Correct answer is **D**.

Question 123:

Which of the following vehicles need to be stopped before crossing a railroad track?

    A. All vehicles where the driver is of an age less than 18 years old

    B. All vehicles with more than four passengers

    C. Trucks with hazardous materials

    D. Pickup trucks used for towing

Correct answer is **C**.

Question 124:

Which of the following signs usually indicates a no-passing zone?

    A. Pentagon shaped signs

    B. Rectangle-shaped signs

    C. Square shaped signs

    D. Pennant shaped signs

Correct answer is **D**.

Question 125:

You are on a single road and see that the approaching driver did not dim the headlights for their vehicle. What should you do?

A. Warn them to dim their lights and get into a fight with them

B. Move your eyes to the right and stop looking at the light to avoid any collisions

C. Stop your car and wait for an officer's assistance

D. Increase the brightness of your vehicle's lights

Correct answer is **B**.

Question 126:

Which of the following statements is true?

A. The stopping distances depend on the speed of the vehicle

B. The stopping distances don't depend on the speed of the vehicle

C. The stopping distances depend on the speed of the vehicle only at night

D. None of the above

Correct answer is **A**.

Question 127:

It would be best not to do this when driving in fog:

A. Following traffic signals

B. Slowing down your speed

C. Observing the surrounding carefully

D. Always on high-beam while driving

Correct answer is **D**.

Explanation:

When driving in fog, it is important to remember that the driver should not use the high-beam light because otherwise, the light will reflect into your eyes and may distract your driving, leading to accidents.

Question 128:

What happens if you continuously break hard while driving on snow?

    A. It will make you cause accidents

    B. It will make the brakes freeze

    C. It will produce heat inside the car

    D. It will cause the front wheels of the vehicle to get locked

Correct answer is **D**.

Question 129:

One of the options can be considered as a driver distraction.

    A. Scanning the vehicles surrounding you

    B. Looking at the signals and signs on the road

    C. Slowing down to glance at a crash scene

    D. Checking if any pedestrians are crossing the road

Correct answer is **C**.

Question 131:

You are almost onto a freeway and your speed is 40 mph. When you reach the end of the ramp you observed that the freeway speed limit is 60 mph. With how much speed must you enter the freeway?

    A. 60 mph

    B. 30 mph

    C. 80 mph

    D. Anything between 50 mph to 100 mph

Correct answer is **A**.

Explanation:

When you enter a freeway, you should always be traveling to the closest speed of the ongoing freeway traffic.

Question 133:

In which of the below conditions do you have the right-of-way?

    A. While coming in the wrong lane

    B. While entering a traffic circle

    C. While already in a traffic circle

    D. All the above

Correct answer is **C**.

Question 134:

Which of the following should be used for communicating with another driver?

    A. Signaling with emergency flashers

    B. Signaling while changing, entering, or exiting lanes

    C. Using horns during emergencies

    D. All the above

Correct answer is **D**.

Question 135:

Which of the below statements is wrong?

    A. You don't need to stop at the STOP sign if there is no traffic

    B. You need to stop at the STOP sign even if there is no traffic

    C. You should not drink alcohol and drive

    D. You should give way to emergency vehicles coming with a siren

Correct answer is **A**.

Question 136:

Near a railroad track, a train has passed. What should you do?

    A. Block the track with your vehicle

    B. If there is a green signal, watch whether any trains are approaching, then proceed with caution

    C. Go on the tracks

    D. Move at the moment you see the green signal

Correct answer is **B**.

Question 137:

Which should you follow if your turn signals are not working?

    A. Emergency flashers

    B. Horning continuously

    C. Use hand signals

    D. Use high-beam headlights

Correct answer is **C**.

Explanation:

If there is any problem with your turn signals or if there is more sunlight that will make your signals not visible for other drivers, it is important to use hand-and-arm signals.

Question 138:

You are in traffic and you see a red traffic light immediately followed by a green arrow in the right direction. What should you do?

    A. Move in the right direction

    B. Move in the left direction

    C. Take a U-turn

    D. Move either in the right or left direction

Correct answer is **A**.

Question 139:

From top to bottom, what is the correct order in a road traffic signal?

A. Green, yellow, red

B. Red, yellow, green

C. Green, red, yellow

D. Yellow, green, red

Correct answer is **B**.

Question 140:

Who of the following should wear seat belts while in a vehicle?

A. Driver

B. Both driver and passengers in the car

C. Only front seat passenger and driver

D. Only back seat passengers

Correct answer is **B**.

Explanation:

Everyone inside the vehicle needs to wear seat belts to prevent injuries during crashes.

Question 141:

You should drive to the right edge of the road and stop during this situation:

A. When you see someone driving rashly

B. When you see someone crossing the lane in a wrong way

C. When you see an emergency vehicle approaching

D. When you see someone driving with alcohol influence

Correct answer is **C**.

Question 142:

What should you do when you pass a bicyclist on the road?

    A. Horn continuously so that the bicyclist will be alerted

    B. Switch on your emergency flashers

    C. Move toward the bicyclist in the center of the lane

    D. Move as far left as possible for safety to the bicyclist

Correct answer is **D**.

Question 143:

One of the below statements is true.

    A. Use high-beam headlights all the time

    B. Use high-beam headlights when it is legal and safe

    C. Use high-beam headlights whenever you are on a highway

    D. Use high-beam headlights only in an emergency

Correct answer is **B**.

Explanation:

High-beam headlights help drivers during different driving conditions. However, it can also cause accidents, especially when it is a single-lane road. Make sure to use high-beam headlights only when it is legal and safe for everyone on the road.

Question 144:

Which one of the following statements is false?

    A. Wearing seatbelts will decrease injuries during traffic crashes

    B. Driving faster will not increase your chances of an accident

    C. Drinking alcohol and driving increases the probability of an accident

    D. When in the middle of an intersection, you will get the right-of-way

Correct answer is **B**.

Question 145:

Out of which of these instances is the road surface the most slippery?

A. After the rain

B. After the snowfall

C. When there is a heavy rain

D. When it just starts to rain

Correct answer is **D**.

Explanation:

During the first signs of rain, the roads will be slippery because the dust and oil on the roads will start to wash away, making the roads slippery. You need to drive more slowly than you usually do during this time as the tires will not get the grip they typically need.

Question 146:

The amount of alcohol in your blood is called:

A. Hemoglobin percentage

B. Blood percentage

C. Blood alcohol percentage

D. All the above

Correct answer is **C**.

Question 147:

Which of the following is true for a driver at an intersection?

A. A driver in the middle of the intersection does not get the right-of-way

B. A driver is not allowed to block an intersection during rush hour

C. A driver is allowed to block an intersection during rush hour

D. A driver at an intersection should completely ignore traffic inspection instructions if given

Correct answer is **B**.

Question 148:

Which of the statements is true about U-turns?

    A.   It is always illegal to make U-turns

    B.   You are allowed to make U-turns only at night

    C.   You are allowed to make U-turns whenever you see a stop signal

    D.   You are allowed to make U-turns at intersections

Correct answer is **D**.

Question 149:

When you drive under the influence of alcohol, one of the below options will be affected:

    A.   Your observation

    B.   Your concentration

    C.   Your coordination

    D.   All the above

Correct answer is **D**.

Question 150:

What happens if a police officer stops you, suspecting that you are under the influence of drugs, and you refuse to take a drug test?

    A.   Your vehicle will be seized

    B.   You will be sent to jail immediately

    C.   You will be asked to pay an additional fine

    D.   Your driving privilege may be taken away from you

Correct answer is **D**.

Question 152:

Which of the following will have a black and orange warning sign?

    A. A service sign

    B. A construction or a maintenance sign

    C. A speed limit sign

    D. A traffic signal ahead sign

Correct answer is **B**.

Question 154:

What will happen if your tire pressure is not inflated to the recommended pressure by your manufacturer?

    A. Your car mileage will increase

    B. Your car can handle slippery roads easily

    C. Improper steering

    D. High gas mileage

Correct answer is **C**.

Question 155:

Which of the following signs can help you navigate an approaching intersection?

    A. Side road sign

    B. Rectangular shape with orange color

    C. Pentagon sign with red color

    D. None of the above

Correct answer is **A**.

Question 156:

Which of the following colors is a sign that tells you the distance of the next exit on a highway?

   A. Blue with red letters

   B. Yellow with blue letters

   C. Green with white letters

   D. Black with white letters

Correct answer is **C.**

Explanation:

All the signs that help you with information about intersecting roads or the roads that can help you make an easy journey are known as guide signs.

Question 157:

You are traveling on the road and you see a sign with "DIP" on it. What does it refer to?

   A. It is a pedestrian ahead warning

   B. It is a sign that says you have to stop immediately

   C. It is a sign that says there is a low place on the road ahead

   D. It is a sign that asks you to increase your speed

Correct answer is **C.**

Explanation:

Whenever you see a DIP sign, you must slow down your vehicle. If not, hydroplaning may occur, leading to you losing control of the vehicle.

Question 158:

For which of the below options is a solid white line mark used?

   A. HOV lanes

   B. Two-way streets

   C. Intersection

   D. Parking lot

Correct answer is **A.**

Question 159:

You are near an intersection and you observe that the green light has changed to yellow. What should you do?

A. Enter the intersection

B. Ask the policeman and do what he says

C. Stop before the intersection

D. Enter the intersection only if it is night

Correct answer is **C**.

Question 160:

You are near an intersection. There is a green light on the signal board and you suddenly hear a fire engine siren from a distance. What should you do?

A. Cross as fast you can before the fire engine comes

B. Stop where you are and wait for the fire engine to pass

C. With full speed, hit the fire engine

D. Cross only if you feel that you have to make an advancement

Correct answer is **B**.

Question 161:

You got involved in an accident and you know that the vehicle needs to be towed away. Within 24 hours, if the law enforcement doesn't appear at the crash scene, what should you do?

A. Wait for the police to appear with patience

B. There is no need for police in this situation

C. Within 24 hours, report the accident to the police station that is close to your residential address

D. Within 24 hours, report the accident to the police station that is near the accident spot

Correct answer is **D**.

Question 162:

Which of the following statements is correct?

A. You should allow pedestrians to cross only if they are children

B. You must allow pedestrians to cross if there is a chance of a collision

C. You should allow pedestrians to cross only if they are adults

D. You should allow pedestrians to cross only if there are marked crossings

Correct answer is **B**.

Explanation:

Horses can be frightened with continuous horning. It is unpredictable to guess how a horse can behave in situations that create anxiety. So, it is important to move your vehicle slowly and give them as much room as you can.

Question 164:

What should you do if an oncoming vehicle's headlights took you by surprise?

A. Stop the car immediately

B. Close your eyes and drive

C. Make sure that you are at the center of the road

D. Slow down until your eyes recover

Correct answer is **D**.

Question 165:

Should you follow temporary traffic lights that are installed at construction sites?

A. No

B. Yes

C. Yes, but only at night

D. Yes, but only when there is rain

Correct answer is **B**.

Question 166:

You are traveling in a vehicle where only the driver's seat has a seatbelt. In this situation, which is a better place to sit?

  A. In the front seat

  B. In the back seat

  C. Share seatbelt along with the driver

  D. Tell the driver to leave and drive yourself

Correct answer is **B**.

Explanation:

If, for some reason, you do not have a seat belt, it is better to sit in the back seat to give yourself better chances of surviving if there is an accident.

Question 167:

What should you do if you see a bus with the sign "give way" on its rear?

  A. Go at normal speed as it is not required to slow down

  B. Honk your horn continuously to alert the bus driver

  C. Slow down and give away for the bus as it has special privilege

  D. None of the above

Correct answer is **C**.

Question 168:

While at a roundabout, what should you do if you decide to take a right turn?

  A. Don't indicate any signal while taking a turn

  B. Indicate right from start to finish

  C. Indicate only if you think it is necessary

  D. Indicate only when you enter the roundabout

Correct answer is **B**.

Question 169:

You need to turn left on the road. When should you use a left-hand indicator?

    A. Only if there is a lot of traffic

    B. Only if there are arrows as signs on the roadway

    C. All the time

    D. Only if it is night

Correct answer is **C**.

Question 170:

Suppose a traffic light has both green and red lights. What does it mean?

    A. The driver can go in any direction

    B. The driver needs to go in the director of red light

    C. The driver can move in the direction of the green arrow

    D. None of the above

Correct answer is **C**.

Question 171:

Which of the following statements is true about carbon monoxide?

    A. You can smell it

    B. You can taste it

    C. It is visible

    D. Inhaling can be fatal

Correct answer is **D**.

Explanation:

Carbon monoxide poisoning is a fatal issue. Carbon monoxide is a poisonous gas and is not visible. Neither can you smell nor taste it. To avoid carbon monoxide poisoning, you need to service the exhaust system regularly.

Question 173:

What is a safety zone?

    A. The middle lane

    B. A space where pedestrians can stay

    C. Place to park cars

    D. Space allocated for high vehicles such as trucks and buses

Correct answer is **B**.

Question 174:

If you sold your car to another person, within how many days do you need to inform the DMV?

    A. Three days

    B. Ten days

    C. Thirty days

    D. Five days

Correct answer is **D**.

Question 175:

If you want to contribute to smoother traffic flow in your community, which of the below options should you follow?

    A. Buy a Tesla

    B. Use a bike

    C. Use public transportation

    D. Stay in the home

Correct answer is **C**.

Question 176:

According to the traffic rules, how many seconds do you need to hand signal before changing lanes?

    A. 10 seconds

    B. 60 seconds

    C. 5 seconds

    D. 2 seconds

Correct answer is **C**.

Question 177:

Which of the following statements is true?

    A. Double parking is not illegal if you are a minor

    B. Double parking is illegal under all circumstances

    C. Double parking is allowed all the time

    D. Double parking is not illegal if you are making a delivery

Correct answer is **B**.

Question 179:

Which might be a probable reason if you have rear-ended the car in front of you?

    A. You are a good driver

    B. You might be following too closely

    C. You are drunk

    D. It is always the other driver's fault

Correct answer is **B**.

Question 180:

Which of the following says that you can stop or park a vehicle for a limited time?

    A. A green painted curb

    B. A yellow painted curb

    C. A red painted curb

    D. A white painted curb

Correct answer is **A**.

Question 181:

You have hit a parked vehicle in an alley. What should you do?

    A. Run as far as you can

    B. Call a lawyer

    C. Call your insurance company

    D. Leave a note with your name and phone number so they can call you and discuss how much you may need to pay for hitting their car

Correct answer is **D**.

Question 182:

You need to be extra careful to look whether any motorcycles are coming while taking turns because:

    A. Motorcyclists are rash drivers

    B. Motorcyclists always drink and drive

    C. It is hard to see them from a long distance often while taking turns due to their small size

    D. All the above

Correct answer is **C**.

Question 183:

You see a signboard with the words "do not pass" on them. What should you do?

    A. You should never pass the sign under any circumstances

    B. You are allowed to pass

    C. You are allowed to pass if you are a child or a senior citizen

    D. You are allowed to pass if you are a government officer

Correct answer is **A**.

Question 184:

You are near a railroad track and you see that the gates are raised for you to pass. With how much speed do you need to pass?

    A. 30 mph

    B. 15 mph

    C. 45 mph

    D. 60 mph

Correct answer is **B**.

Question 185:

You should never park:

    A. In a parking space

    B. In front of rest stops

    C. In a space that is marked with a no-hatch pattern

    D. Hundred feet away from a railroad track

Correct answer is **C**.

Question 186:

You are continuously violating traffic rules. What may happen?

    A. Your insurance will be revoked

    B. Your family members will be alerted

    C. You may lose your driving privilege

    D. You will be given an award

Correct answer is **C**.

Question 187:

When should you use a turn-out lane?

    A. When you are bored of driving

    B. When you want to make a U-turn

    C. When faster drivers want to pass you

    D. When you give way to emergency vehicles

Correct answer is **C**.

Question 189:

You need to signal while making a turn before how many feet?

    A. 30 feet

    B. 50 feet

    C. 100 feet

    D. 200 feet

Correct answer is **C**.

Question 190:

You need at least a how many second gap in oncoming traffic to pass the car ahead of you when driving at 50 mph on a two-lane road?

    A. 10 to 12 seconds

    B. 1 second

    C. 5 seconds

    D. 3 seconds

Correct answer is **A**.

Question 191:

A curb is painted in red. What does it mean?

- A. It means that you can park there
- B. It means that you need to alert a police officer whenever you see that paint
- C. It means that it is for disabled persons
- D. It means that stopping or parking is not allowed there

Correct answer is **D**.

Question 192:

What should you do if your vehicle breaks down in the middle of the road and you sense that it may obstruct traffic flow?

- A. Switch on hazard warning signals
- B. Switch on your parking signals
- C. Honk your horn continuously
- D. Stop your car suddenly on the road and walk away

Correct answer is **A**.

Question 193:

You are a driver with a vision problem. What should you do?

- A. Drive as usual
- B. Drive with your eyes closed
- C. Drive only when you wear prescribed optical glasses
- D. Drive only after wearing contact lenses or optical glasses that improve your vision while driving

Correct answer is **D**.

Question 194:

Who of the following are vulnerable road users?

    A. Pedestrians

    B. Bicyclists

    C. Horse riders

    D. All the above

Correct answer is **D**.

Explanation:

It is important to give way to vulnerable road users whenever they are trying to cross the road. You need to make sure that you provide enough room for them. Your lack of judgment can affect their lives, so have some courtesy.

Question 195:

Children can be considered as vulnerable road users because:

    A. They are unpredictable

    B. They don't usually know about road rules

    C. They are mischievous

    D. They close their eyes while moving on roads

Correct answer is **A**.

Question 196:

What should you do when you see older people crossing the road?

    A. Honk the horn continuously to scare them

    B. Be patient and let them cross

    C. Take a U-turn

    D. Get out and shout at them to cross faster

Correct answer is **B**.

Question 197:

What should you do when you see a sign with an airplane on it?

A. It indicates that there is an airport nearby

B. It means that planes move at low heights in the area

C. It means that you need to stop immediately

D. It means that you need to change roads

Correct answer is **B**.

Question 198:

What should you do when you smell petrol while driving?

A. Drive as fast as you can

B. Light a matchstick

C. Stop the car and investigate

D. Ignore the smell

Correct answer is **C**.

Question 199:

What will happen when you enter a tunnel?

A. Visibility will decrease

B. You will get improved driving skills

C. The space will increase

D. It will rain

Correct answer is **A**.

Question 200:

Which of the following options do you need to be aware of to be a good driver?

A. Other vehicles on the road

B. Weather conditions

C. Signs and signals

D. All the above

Correct answer is **D**.

Question 201:

Why are mirrors on vehicles?

    A. To help you know how your actions on the road can affect the vehicles behind you

    B. To help other drivers see

    C. To help you comb your hair

    D. To help bicyclists and motorcyclists

Correct answer is **A**.

Question 202:

Which of the following can you not see from your mirror?

    A. Cars behind you

    B. Trucks behind you

    C. Blindspots

    D. Bicyclist behind you

Correct answer is **C**.

Question 204:

Which of the following is considered a better idea?

    A. If you are unable to reverse your car, leave it right there

    B. If you are unable to reverse your car, ask someone to guide you to reverse safely

    C. If you are unable to reverse your car, inform a police officer

    D. If you are unable to reverse your car, honk your horn continuously

Correct answer is **B**.

Question 205:

Which of these should be followed while driving?

    A. Make sure to wear seat belts

    B. Make sure to hand signal whenever crossing lanes

    C. If your view is blocked because of any parked cars near a junction, make sure that you move slowly and proceed only when you have a clear view

    D. All the above

Correct answer is **D**.

Question 206:

Which of the following is more important when you are trying to overtake a vehicle?

    A. Your age

    B. Your observation

    C. Your BAC

    D. Your driving experience

Correct answer is **B**.

Question 207:

What should you do at night when you are at a point of a bridge where you can't be seen by the driver coming from the other side?

    A. Use the horn

    B. Take a U-turn and go from another route

    C. Switch on high-beam headlights

    D. Move slowly without making any noise

Correct answer is **A**.

Question 208:

Which of the following statements is true?

- A. Hazards never occur on roads
- B. You need to break to stay safe on the road constantly
- C. If you are unable to see the mirrors of a large vehicle, then it is more probable that the large vehicle's driver is unable to see you
- D. Construction signs should usually be ignored

Correct answer is **C**.

Question 209:

Road signs are present to:

- A. Help you improve your comprehension skills
- B. Help you avoid problems and drive safely
- C. Help you gain knowledge
- D. Help you realize your driving skills

Correct answer is **B**.

Question 210:

Which of the following conditions can affect your driving or influence how you anticipate what might happen?

- A. Poor light
- B. Bad weather
- C. High traffic
- D. All the above

Correct answer is **D**.

Question 211:

What can help you keep control of your vehicle?

    A. Listening to music while driving

    B. Keeping both hands on the wheel while your brake

    C. Reading traffic boards

    D. Looking at other vehicles

Correct answer is **B**.

Question 212:

Which of the following can help you to stay focused?

    A. Reading books while driving

    B. Listening to audiobooks while driving

    C. Having regular stops while driving

    D. None of the above

Correct answer is **C**.

Question 213:

It is usually not recommended to drive continuously for more than:

    A. Six hours

    B. Eight hours

    C. Twelve hours

    D. Two hours

Correct answer is **D**.

Question 214:

Which of the following is a short-term substitute if you feel drowsy?

    A. Taking caffeinated drinks such as coffee

    B. Drinking alcohol

    C. Using marijuana

    D. Driving with your eyes closed

Correct answer is **A**.

Question 215:

Which of the following options is illegal?

A. Using a mobile phone while driving

B. Driving without a seat belt

C. Driving way above the speed limit

D. All the above

Correct answer is **D**.

Question 216:

Safe driving will only be possible:

A. If your vehicle is a high-end car

B. If your vehicle is an electric car

C. If your vehicle has a high-level accelerator

D. If the driver is alert and focused while driving

Correct answer is **D**.

Question 217:

What should you do if a large vehicle is trying to overtake you?

A. Slow down and let it pass

B. Block the road so that it cannot overtake you

C. Go as fast as you can

D. Slow down and let it pass only if there is more traffic

Correct answer is **A**.

Question 218:

You should honk your horn only when:

A. There is a danger or an emergency

B. You are impatient

C. You are drowsy

D. You are hungry

Correct answer is **A**.

Question 219:

Why are headlights flashed mostly at night?

    A. To help drivers drive better

    B. To help drivers make decisions

    C. To help other drivers know that you are there

    D. To see how the traffic is ahead

Correct answer is **C.**

Question 220:

What should you do if animals such as sheep are on the road?

    A. Stop your car and wait for a police officer

    B. Stop your car and switch off your engine until you are sure that the road is clear

    C. Take a U-turn

    D. Make them scared by honking the horn so they will leave

Correct answer is **B.**

Question 221:

Tailgating is considered as a:

    A. Driving skill that needs to be learned by everyone who drives

    B. Very dangerous act as it can cause collisions if the vehicle in front stops suddenly

    C. Defensive driving skill

    D. Not so distracting act for the driver of the front vehicle

Correct answer is **B.**

Question 222:

During bad weather conditions, the distance between two vehicles should at least have a:

A. Six-second gap

B. Four-second gap

C. Ten-second gap

D. One-second gap

Correct answer is **B**.

Question 223:

At unmarked crossroads, who has more priority?

A. Cars

B. Motorcycles

C. Buses

D. No one

Correct answer is **D**.

Question 224:

Following large vehicles such as trucks and buses is unsafe because:

A. You may have to drive slowly

B. Your road view will be smaller, making it unsafe

C. It is not legal

D. None of the above

Correct answer is **B**.

Question 225:

At least for how many months do you need to service your vehicle?

A. 2 months

B. 6 months

C. 12 months

D. 24 months

Correct answer is **A**.

Question 226:

What can under-inflated tires cause?

    A. Increase your stopping distance

    B. Improve your driving

    C. Make you take U-turns easily

    D. Helps you to overtake easily

Correct answer is **A**.

Question 227:

Which of the following statements is true?

    A. You need to top up your battery with distilled water from time to time

    B. You need to check the oil and coolant levels before a long journey

    C. Ensure that the brake fluid is not low

    D. All the above

Correct answer is **D**.

Question 228:

Which of the following is illegal?

    A. Driving without alcohol influence

    B. Stopping your vehicle when you hear and see a red siren

    C. Driving without listening to music

    D. Driving with tires that have cuts or defects in the side walls

Correct answer is **D**.

Question 229:

What is dry steering?

    A. Turning the steering wheel while driving

    B. Turning the steering wheel at night

    C. Turning the steering wheel when it is raining

    D. Turning the steering wheel while the car isn't moving

Correct answer is **D**.

Explanation:

It is not recommended to dry steer because it may cause damage to the tires, leading to accidents.

Question 230:

What is the purpose of an anti-lock braking system (ABS)?

    A. To help wheels move fast

    B. To help prevent wheel lockup

    C. To help other drivers alert that your brakes are damaged

    D. To help all wheels to lockup

Correct answer is **B**.

Explanation:

An anti-lock braking system is used to prevent the vehicle wheels from being locked up. If the ABS warning doesn't go off when the vehicle is moving at 5-10 mph, it means that a qualified mechanic should check the ABS.

Question 231:

What should you do if a brake fade happens?

    A. Stop using brakes

    B. Honk your horn continuously

    C. Use a lower gear to help control the vehicle speed

    D. Start to use higher gear to help control the vehicle speed

Correct answer is **C**.

Explanation:

Brake fade happens when the brakes become less effective because of overheating. Overheating may occur when you use them continuously.

Question 232:

What should you do if the steering wheel vibrates while you are driving?

    A. Visit a mechanic for assistance

    B. Drive normally

    C. Drive fast

    D. Drive slowly

Correct answer is **A**.

Explanation:

The steering wheel vibrates when the wheels are not balanced. It is important to adjust the wheels and tires to reduce any vibrations in the vehicle.

Question 233:

While traveling, children between 3 to 12 years old should use a:

    A. Phone

    B. Adult seatbelts

    C. Suitable child restraint

    D. None of the above

Correct answer is **C**.

Explanation:

It is important that children use a suitable child restraint. If a child restraint is not available, then in the rear seat, children should be using an adult seat belt. However, this should be done only during emergencies.

Question 234:

While traveling, children under three years old should use a:

    A. Child restraint

    B. Adult seatbelt

    C. Suitable child seat

    D. The driver's lap

Correct answer is **C**.

Question 235:

What should you do when you enter a car?

    A. Adjust the seat in a way that you can control the steering comfortably

    B. Adjust the head restraint to avoid any neck injuries if there is a collision

    C. Adjust the mirrors in a way that you can see all vehicles around you

    D. All the above

Correct answer is **D**.

Question 236:

In which of these instances can you switch on the hazard lights?

- A. When your car has broken down
- B. When you want to have fun
- C. When you see an emergency vehicle coming
- D. When you are crossing lanes

Correct answer is **A**.

Question 237:

Which of the following statements is wrong?

- A. Use hazard signals while parking
- B. Use emergency lights while parking
- C. Use high-beam lights while parking
- D. All the above

Correct answer is **D**.

Explanation:

It is not recommended to use hazard, emergency, or high-beam lights while parking. Use a parking signal or hand signal to help other drivers understand that you are trying to park your car.

Question 238:

Which of the following is recommended not to let someone steal your car?

- A. Write a note to the driver to not steal it
- B. Keep car keys with you and lock your car
- C. Use a steering lock
- D. Ask someone to watch your car

Correct answer is **C**.

Explanation:

A steering lock is a visible anti-theft device that, as the name implies, immobilizes the steering wheel of a car.

Question 239:

Which of the following is considered wrong?

    A.   Switching on the car engine and locking your car before leaving

    B.   Giving hand signals while changing lanes

    C.   Not tailgating other vehicles

    D.   Using mirrors to observe the vehicles behind you

Correct answer is **A**.

Question 240:

Which of the following places do you need to avoid parking?

    A.   Near a bus stop

    B.   In front of an entrance

    C.   At a pedestrian crossing

    D.   All the above

Correct answer is **D**.

Question 241:

Which of the following guidelines do you need to use to make your driving safe?

    A.   Go with high speed

    B.   Do rapid acceleration

    C.   Always heavy brake

    D.   Use selective gear changing

Correct answer is **D**.

Question 242:

Which of the following should not be encouraged while driving?

    A. Carrying unnecessary loads on the top of your car

    B. Driving slowly near a school zone

    C. Giving way to pedestrians when they are stuck on the road while crossing

    D. Using low-beam headlights at night while traveling

Correct answer is **A**.

Question 243:

To avoid traffic congestion leading to stress, which of the following options should be followed?

    A. Plan what route you will be traveling beforehand

    B. Don't plan your journey

    C. Always drive at busy times

    D. Take U-turns and disobey traffic rules whenever possible

Correct answer is **A**.

Question 244:

Which of the following options can be considered a good way to plan your route?

    A. Using satellite equipment such as a GPS

    B. Following a route planner that will be available on the Internet for frequent travelers

    C. Looking at a map that provides info about different routes

    D. All the above

Correct answer is **D**.

Question 245:

Which of the following is true?

   A.   Thinking distance + braking distance = stopping distance

   B.   Thinking distance = stopping distance

   C.   Braking distance = stopping distance

   D.   None of the above

Correct answer is **A**.

Explanation:

Thinking distance is often known as the distance that a driver travels within the time they react to a situation, and the braking distance is referred to as the distance that is traveled when you start to use brakes as a reaction to the situation. The combined time is known as the stopping distance.

Question 246:

How many seconds should there be between two vehicles in icy weather?

   A.   3 seconds

   B.   2 seconds

   C.   20 seconds

   D.   5 seconds

Correct answer is **C**.

Question 247:

Which of the following will have a major effect on your safety margins?

   A.   Following signs and signals

   B.   Weather conditions

   C.   Wearing a seat belt

   D.   Not tailgating

Correct answer is **B**.

Question 248:

When there is a lot of rain while driving, which of the following can happen?

    A. Faster speeds

    B. Hydroplaning

    C. Roads becoming smooth

    D. None of the above

Correct answer is **B**.

Question 249:

Hot weather can be dangerous for drivers because:

    A. You will lose your energy while driving

    B. Road surface becomes soft and can melt sometimes. This can affect your steering and braking

    C. You will become drowsy

    D. You will become over-energetic

Correct answer is **B**.

Question 250:

When there is bright sunlight, the other drivers cannot see:

    A. Your face

    B. Your mirror

    C. Your windshield

    D. Your indicators flashing

Correct answer is **D**.

Question 251:

What should you do if your windshield wipers are not working because of snow stuck between them?

    A. Move with an unclear view

    B. Pull over and stop your car to clear the wipers using your hand

    C. Take a U-turn and go to a mechanic

    D. Honk continuously while driving with an unclear view

Correct answer is **B**.

Question 252:

To whom should you give space when there is a high wind?

    A. Cyclists

    B. Motorcyclists

    C. High-loaded vehicles

    D. All the above

Correct answer is **D**.

Question 253:

Why does skidding occur?

    A. Skidding occurs when you drive while drunk

    B. Skidding occurs when the tires lose grip on the road

    C. Skidding occurs when the driver is a minor

    D. Skidding only occurs when there are bad weather conditions

Correct answer is **B**.

Question 254:

To reduce the risk of skidding:

- A. You need to constantly scan the road to observe any signs or signals that mention the condition of the roads
- B. Make sudden steering movements
- C. Do hard braking
- D. Always drive with the lowest gear

Correct answer is **A**.

Question 255:

What is a hazard?

- A. A hazard is where you need to wait for a police officer to come
- B. A hazard is a situation where you as a driver need to take action by steering or braking to avoid any accidents
- C. A hazard is a situation when you need to make a U-turn
- D. A hazard is a situation when you need to call 911

Correct answer is **B**.

Question 256:

Hazards can usually be:

- A. Static hazards such as parked cars and roundabouts
- B. Moving hazards such as pedestrians or bicyclists
- C. Caused by you
- D. All the above

Correct answer is **D**.

Explanation:

As a driver, you need to expect hazards from anywhere. Hazards can be static that are caused by parked cars or because of junctions. Hazards can be moving when crossing pedestrians or drunk bicyclists cause them. In some situations, hazards can also be caused by you when you are either tired or drunk. A good driver always sees the dangers and acts responsibly so that there won't be any accidents.

Question 257:

Which of the following is a static hazard?

   A. Junctions

   B. Moving pedestrians

   C. You being drunk while driving

   D. Horse riders

Correct answer is **A**.

Question 258:

Why are there road signs on the road?

   A. To help drivers know about the possible hazards

   B. To help drivers go quickly to their destination

   C. To help drivers carefully drive when drunk

   D. To help drivers stop time

Correct answer is **A**.

Question 259:

Which of the following is a possible hazard because of parked vehicles?

   A. Vehicles moving with fast speed

   B. Vehicles' doors opening suddenly

   C. Vehicles taking a U-turn

   D. All the above

Correct answer is **B**

Question 260:

What does this sign represent?

A. A STOP sign

B. A speed limit sign

C. A sign that says that you should make a U-turn

D. A sign that says that you can move forward

Correct answer is **A**.

Explanation:

A STOP sign is used to warn drivers that they need to stop their vehicles immediately. This can either be on a traffic signal, signboard, or sometimes even in the hand of an officer. There are one-way stops, two-ways stops, and four-way stops. For example, if there are stop boards for north and west traffic, the ongoing traffic on south and east does not need to stop.

Question 261:

What should you do when you see the below sign?

A. Stop your vehicle

B. Honk your horn continuously

C. Move forward without stopping in the middle

D. Check the oncoming traffic and if there is no oncoming traffic then proceed

Correct answer is **D**.

Explanation:

This sign is called a yield sign. When you see a yield sign while driving, you need to check for oncoming traffic. If you are sure that no one is coming, you can proceed. If there is oncoming traffic, you must stop there and wait for the traffic to clear.

Question 262:

When you see a "do not enter" sign, what should you do?

A. Do not enter the street under any circumstances

B. Enter the street

C. Enter the street only if you have an electric vehicle

D. Do not enter the street when there is no light

Correct answer is **A**.

Explanation:

"Do not enter - Wrong way" signboards are usually posted on one-way streets where they have an exit or entrance to a highway. When you see this sign, it is important not to enter the road in any circumstances as you will be changing the traffic flow and may cause crashes. Not following the signboard and entering the street can lead to hefty fines.

Question 263:

What does this sign represent?

A. That you can travel in two directions

B. That you can travel in only one direction, the direction that the arrow is pointed

C. That you can travel in only one direction, opposite the direction that the arrow is pointed

D. None of the above

Correct answer is **B**.

Explanation:

One-way signs are regulatory signs that help drivers understand the direction of the traffic. You should never travel in the opposite direction of the arrow shown because it will increase the risk of a head-on collision. You will usually find one-way signs during intersections and T-intersections.

Question 264:

What should you do when you see this sign?

A. Do not cross the speed that is mentioned on the signboard

B. Always cross the speed that is mentioned on the signboard

C. Maintain the mentioned speed when only on highways

D. Maintain the mentioned speed only when on rural roads

Correct answer is **A**.

Explanation:

Speed limit signs are present to help control the flow of the traffic. It is important to follow these signs when you are driving and to not go way above or below the speed limit. Both slow drivers and fast drivers can be a problem for traffic flow. For example, if the speed limit on the signboard is 65 mph, you can maintain a speed between 60-65 mph for smoother flow.

Question 265:

What does this sign with a red marker on the truck symbol represent?

A. It means that trucks are allowed

B. It means that trucks are not allowed

C. It means that trucks are allowed at night

D. None of the above

Correct answer is **B**.

Explanation:

When you see a no truck signal, you need to ensure that there are no large vehicles behind you. Warning them also can help not to cause further problems along the road.

Question 266:

What does this sign with a red marker on a bicycle represent?

A. That bicycles are not allowed

B. That bicycles are allowed

C. That bicycles are allowed only in the center lane

D. That bicycles are allowed only in the left lane

Correct answer is **A**.

Explanation:

When you see a no bicycle signal, you need to make sure that no bicycles are entering along with you. Warning them with hand signals or hazard signals can help to not cause further problems along the road.

Question 267:

What does this sign with a red marker on a person represent?

    A. That people are not allowed on that particular road

    B. That it is a road constructed for animals

    C. That people should not cross the road at this intersection

    D. That people can cross the road at this intersection

Correct answer is **C**.

Explanation:

This sign is used to help have a smoother traffic flow during an intersection as it prohibits pedestrians from crossing the intersections.

Question 268:

What does this sign with a red marker represent?

    A. That you are allowed to make Returns

    B. That you are allowed to make U-turns only if you are a minor

    C. That you are not allowed to make Returns

    D. That you are allowed to make U-turns when there is no traffic

Correct answer is **C**.

Question 269:

What does this sign with a red marker on the "P" letter represent?

A. It is a no parking sign

B. It means you can park only two-wheel vehicles here

C. You can stop your car here only for a few minutes

D. You can park your car until you see an officer

Correct answer is **A.**

Explanation:

A no parking sign is used to help drivers understand that they cannot park their vehicles where a no parking sign is placed, even for a short time. If an officer finds a vehicle by a no parking sign, they may tow it to the station and after paying hefty fines, will you be able to receive your vehicle again.

Question 270:

What does this sign represent?

A. That it is safe to pass

B. It is safe to pass when wearing your seatbelt

C. That it is safe to pass when it is raining

D. That you are in a no-passing zone

Correct answer is **D**.

Explanation:

When you see a "do not pass" sign, it is important to understand that it is illegal to pass a car going in the same direction. This sign is used when there are high chances of unforeseen hazards such as hills, deep curves, and intersections.

Question 271:

What does this sign with a curved right arrow and the word "only" represent?

A. It means that the vehicles in your lane should turn only right at the intersection

B. It means that the vehicles in your lane should not turn right at the intersection

C. It means that you need to make a U-turn

D. It means that you need to honk your horn continuously while taking a right turn near the intersection

Correct answer is **B**.

Question 272:

What does this sign with the words 'keep right' represent?

A. It means that you need to take a right turn

B. It means that you need to always stay right of the traffic divider

C. It means that you need to stay left to the traffic divider

D. It means that you need to randomly move to different lanes while driving

Correct answer is **B**.

Question 273:

What does this sign with the words "reserved parking" represent?

A. That you can park your car

B. That you can park your car only if you are disabled

C. That you can park your car at night

D. That you can park your car while it is raining

Correct answer is **B**.

Explanation:

To park in a reserved parking spot, you need an authorized license plate. Otherwise, you may get a fine.

Question 274:

What does this sign represent?

A. That drivers should be aware that there is a school in the area

B. That drivers should move slowly to not cause any accidents or collisions with children

C. That drivers should yield to children if they are trying to cross the road

D. All the above

Correct answer is **D**.

Explanation:

A school zone is special as many children will be trying to cross the roads. As a driver, it is your responsibility to make sure that you are aware of the surroundings and be alert because children may come onto the streets all of a sudden.

Question 275:

What does this sign with a number represent?

A. These are regular speed signs

B. These are not speed signs but represent the interstate highway

C. These are advisory speed signs

D. These are signs that mention how far the next city is

Correct answer is **C**.

Question 276:

What does this sign represent?

    A. A two-way stop

    B. A four-way stop

    C. A three-way stop

    D. A six-way stop

Correct answer is **A**.

Question 277:

What does this sign with a "Y" shape represent?

    A. Two roads will become a single road

    B. Two roads will split from a single road

    C. That the road will end

    D. Road will divide into three roads

Correct answer is **B**.

Question 278:

What does this sign with an arrowed circle represent?

A. It means that there is an intersection ahead

B. It means that there is a traffic circle ahead

C. It means that there is a roundabout ahead

D. It means that there is a road ahead

Correct answer is **B**.

Explanation:

Traffic circles are usually present to slow down the flow of traffic.

Question 279:

What do the signs that you will see around tunnels and overpasses represent?

A. It helps you understand that there will be no lights ahead

B. It helps you understand that the structures will usually have a low ceiling

C. It helps you understand that you need to go two times more than your regular speed

D. It helps you understand that you do not need to follow traffic rules ahead

Correct answer is **B**.

Question 280:

What does this sign represent?

    A. That the roads ahead have more curves

    B. That the roads ahead are slippery

    C. That the roads ahead need to have high speeds

    D. That the roads ahead are not slippery

Correct answer is **B**.

Question 281:

What does this sign with a truck represent?

    A. That you are on a steep hill and hence, you need to slow down

    B. That you are entering uphill

    C. That only trucks are allowed

    D. That you need to completely switch off your vehicle

Correct answer is **A**.

Question 282:

What does this sign represent?

A. It says that you need to stop immediately

B. It says that there is a stop sign ahead

C. It says that you need to make a U-turn

D. It says that you need to slow down for the rest of your journey

Correct answer is **B**.

Question 283:

What does this sign represent?

A. It means that you need not to follow traffic signals ahead

B. It means that there is a traffic signal ahead in the next intersection

C. It means that you need to call a police officer

D. None of the above

Correct answer is **B**.

Question 284:

What does this sign with a bicycle represent?

   A.   That the road is allowed only for bicycles

   B.   That there are frequent bicycle users at the intersection

   C.   That you need to follow road rules only when there is a bicycle

   D.   That you don't need to follow road rules when there is a bicycle

Correct answer is **B**.

Question 285:

What does this sign with two "R's" represent?

   A.   That you will need to cross a railroad further ahead

   B.   That you need to stop your vehicle immediately

   C.   That you need to cross the railroad tracks with high speed

   D.   None of the above

Correct answer is **A**.

Question 286:

What does this sign with a person represent?

A. That there is a crosswalk ahead and there will be pedestrians trying to cross the road

B. That there is a crosswalk ahead

C. That you can move as fast as you can

D. That you should stop immediately

Correct answer is **A**.

Question 287:

What does this sign with a horse represent?

A. It means that this road is only for horses

B. It means that the road is often frequented with horse carriages and horse riders

C. It means that you need to make a U-turn

D. It means that the road is closed

Correct answer is **B**.

Question 288:

What does this sign represent?

A. It means that the road is not functioning

B. It means that you can cross the road only at night

C. It means that the road has active road construction

D. All the above

Correct answer is **C**.

Conclusion

We are glad that you have reached the end of the book. You have done well and now all you need to do is attend the exam as per your appointment and attempt it! All the best!

How to Not Become Anxious During the Exam Day

It is common for people to become panicked when there is an exam. For people trying to ace the DMV test, panic can be a bad thing because it affects your score and may result in not getting your license. There is no substitution for hard work. It would be best to prepare a few weeks before reading this section. Remember, without sufficient hard work and solving any exercises or writing mock tests beforehand, it isn't easy to pass the test. Even though the DMV test is more testing towards your common sense and knowledge related to the road rules, you still need to be completely free of the burden to perform better in the test.

1. Learn How to Study Efficiently

    To perform better, you need to study efficiently. Simple rote learning can lead you nowhere. Understand what you are reading and try to express them in your own words to understand their real essence. The passive recall method can help you remember the content more vividly, boosting your confidence, and eliminating anxiety.

2. Study Early

    To perform better at tests without worrying about the results, make sure to start preparing many days before the actual exam. For example, if you are scheduled to write your exam in January, start preparing at least from November to ensure that you will have a good chance of cracking the exam.

3. Establish a Consistent Pretest Routine

    We recommend establishing a consistent pretest routine to beat the exam without being anxious on the test day. Routine mock tests will help you deal with the real exam you are trying to pass. Either attend online tests or revise the content by hiding the answers. Don't forget to give the same time you usually take for each question during the real exam.

4. Learn Relaxation Techniques

    Relaxation techniques are a great way to boost your confidence and help you ace the exam without anxiety. We recommend meditation and breathing exercises for better results. Always do a couple of "deep in - deep out" breathing exercises when you enter the exam hall. Breathing exercises will help to relieve stress. Doing a meditation session a few hours before the exam can also help you to do better as your mind will be free during these sessions.

5. Have a Good Night Sleep

    It is always recommended to have a good night's sleep the day before the exam date. Enough sleep will help you to think clearly during the exam. Pulling an all-nighter the day before the exam and expecting to pass is not a great idea, especially for an exam like DMV.

6. Get Some Exercise

    Physical exercises will also help your body's hormones to function effectively during the exam. No physical movement is a bad thing for your brain functioning. On the exam day, have a small jog near a park or on your balcony. It will feel better to attempt an exam when you start your day with a good exercise that bends your muscles and increases your cognitive energy.

7. Have Positive Thoughts

    Before writing the exam, you must have positive thoughts about the result. Imagine that you have passed the test and the results will follow. There is nothing better than filling yourself up with positive energy before writing an exam.

We hope you will do well in the exam. Remember that failures are common, and even though we are sure that you can pass the test easily with our well-written guide, we still want you to be hopeful and stay hungry for the next attempt in any adverse situation. There is nothing better than trying. We wish you all the best. We hope you will be a great driver by following the rules and being accountable for yourself!

References

All images sourced from shutterstock.
https://www.shutterstock.com/image-vector/over-three-hundred-fifty-different-highly-127200926

Made in the USA
Las Vegas, NV
23 May 2022